# THE LAW OF GIVING
# &
# RECEIVING

"Give, and it shall be given unto you...;"

**Luke6:38**

By
Franklin N. Abazie

# *The Law of Giving and Receiving*

COPYRIGHT 2018 BY Franklin N Abazie
ISBN: 978-1-945-133-800

All right reserved. This book or any portion thereof may not be reproduced or used in any manner whatsoever without the express written permission of the publisher, except for the use of brief quotations in a book review. All Bible quotes are from King James Version and others as noted.

Published by:  F N ABAZIE PUBLISHING HOUSE---
a.k.a,
Empowerment Bookstore:

That I may publish with the voice of thanksgiving and tell of all thy wondrous works. **Psalms26:7**

To order additional copies, wholesales or booking: Call the Church office (973-372-7518)
or Empowerment Bookstore Hotline 973-393-8518
Worship address:
343 Sanford Avenue Newark New Jersey 07106
Administrative Head Office address:
33 Schley Street Newark New Jersey 07112
Email:pastorfranknto@yahoo.com
Website www.fnabaziehealingministries.org
Publishing House: www.fnabaziepublishinghouse.org

This book is a production of F N Abazie Publishing House.

A publication Arms of Miracle of God Ministries 2018
First Edition

# CONTENTS

THE MANDATE OF THE COMMISSION............iv

ARMS OF THE COMMISSION...............................v

INTRODUCTION....................................................viii

CHAPTER 1

1. The Grace to Give ...............................................48

CHAPTER 2

2. The Power to Receive..........................................64

CHAPTER 3

3. Prayer of Salvation..............................................87

CHAPTER 4

4. About the Author.................................................97

# *THE MANDATE OF THE COMMISSION*

"THE MOMENT IS DUE TO IMPACT YOUR WORLD THROUGH THE REVIVAL OF THE HEALING & MIRACLE MINISTRY OF JESUS CHRIST OF NAZARETH.

I AM SENDING YOU TO RESTORE HEALTH UNTO THEE AND I WILL HEAL THEE OF THY WOUNDS, SAID THE LORD OF HOST."

# *ARMS OF THE COMMISSION*

1) F N Abazie Ministries-Miracle of God Ministries (Miracle Chapel Intl)

2) F N Abazie TV Ministries: Global Television Ministry Outreach.

3) F N Abazie Radio Ministries: Radio Broadcasting Outreach.

4) F N Abazie Publishing House: Book Publication.

5) F N Abazie Bible School: also called Word of Healing Bible School (W.O.H.B.S)

6) F N Abazie Evangelistic Ass: Miracle of God Ministries: Global Crusade

7) Empowerment Bookstore: Book distribution.

8) F N Abazie Helping Hands: Meeting the help of the needy world wide

9) F N Abazie Disaster Recovery Mission: Global Disaster Recovery.

10) F N Abazie Prison Ministry: Prison Ministry for all convicts "Second chance"

**Some of our ministry arms are waiting the appointed time to commence**

# *FAVOR CONFESSION*

*Father thank you for making me righteous and accepted through the blood of Jesus Christ. Because of that, I am blessed and highly favored by God. I am the subject of your affection. Your favor surrounds me as a shield, and the first thing that people see around me is your favored shield.*

*Thank you that I have favor with you and man today. All day long people go out of their way to bless me and help me. I have favor with everyone that I deal with today. Doors that were once closed are now opened for me. I receive preferential treatment, and I have special privileges, I am Gods favored child.*

*No good thing will he withhold from me. Because of Gods favor my enemies cannot triumph over my life. I have supernatural increase and promotion. I declare restoration to everything that the devil has stolen from my life. I have honor in the midst of my adversaries and an increase in assets, especially in real estate and expansion of*

*Because I am highly favored by God, I experience great victories, supernatural turnarounds, and miraculous breakthrough in the midst of great impossibilities. I receive recognition, prominence, and honor. Petitions are granted to me even by ungodly authorities. Policies, rules, regulations, and laws are changed and reverse on my behalf.*

*I win battles that I don't even have to fight, because God fights them for me. This is the day, the set time and the designated moment for me to experience the free favor of God, that profusely and lavishly abound on my behalf in Jesus name. Amen.*

# **INTRODUCTION**

The law of *Giving* and *Receiving* is a book that teaches us how to *give* and how to *receive*, both from God & man. *It takes the Grace of God to Give and to Receive.* Most of us do not know how these principles work.

I prayed over a man who was going through a few family and financial challenges, he gave an offering into our ministry, and a few weeks later, he requested back for his free will offering, I have never witnessed such a thing in my life until I encountered this fellow. The below scripture says *"While the earth remaineth, seedtime and harvest, and cold and heat, and summer and winter, and day and night shall not cease.*

*"While the earth remaineth, seedtime and harvest, and cold and heat, and summer and winter, and day and night shall not cease."*
**Genesis8:22**

Although it takes the *Grace* of God to *give and to receive*, we must always develop a humble, and liberal heart that is acceptable unto God, if we must give or receive anything good in life.

Most of us do not know how these spiritual things work.

*It will interest me for you to understand what we are saying*, these are spiritual principles that can never be broken. That is, no matter how logical, and smart, we think we are, *"seedtime and harvest shall not cease."*

The bible says *"And let us not be weary in well doing: for in due season we shall reap, if we faint not."* Often, we try to out-smart the next guy with our rational, and logical reasoning, like the guy in my story above, who requested a refund of his offering.

Whatever you sow in life, you shall reap in due time. Some of us, do not pay tithes or give an offering to support God's work, yet we want to be mightily blessed.

The Lord said, *"My covenant will I not break, nor alter the thing that is gone out of my lips."* I encourage you to appreciate the truth. Unless we embrace the teaching's on *giving*, we will never be positioned good enough to *receive* in life.

Happy Reading!

# HIS DESTINY WAS THE CROSS....

# HIS PURPOSE WAS LOVE.....

# HIS REASON WAS YOU....

"But as many as received him, to them gave he power to become the sons of God, even to them that believe on his name"

## John1:12

# Prayer points

*"If ye shall ask any thing in my name, I will do it.."*
**John14:14**

Holy Spirit of God frustrate and disappoint, every one that is against my life and family, in the name of Jesus.

Father Lord destroy every demonic networks and traps against my progress in life in the name of Jesus.

Fire of God, destroy every demonic projection and curses against my life and destiny in the name of Jesus.

Every spell and curses pronounced against my destiny, break, in the name of Jesus.

Hand of God cage every power militating against my rising in life, in the name of Jesus.

God silent every voice raising a counter motion against my elevation, in the mighty name of Jesus.

Blood of Jesus neutralize every spirit of Balaam hired to hinder my life, ministry, and career, the name of Jesus.

Fire of God destroy every curse that I have brought into my life through ignorance and disobedience, break by fire, in the name of Jesus.

Ancient of day destroy every power harassing my ministry in the name of Jesus.

Father God deliver me from invincible forces militating against my life and destiny.

Power of God frustrate every coven and demonic network, designed to frustrate and hinder my success in life, in the name of Jesus.

I dismantle every strong hold designed to imprison my talent in the mighty name of Jesus.

I reject every cycle of frustration, in the name of Jesus.

Power of God paralyze every agent assigned to frustrate my life in the name of Jesus.

Finger of God, grant me supernatural speed against all my contenders in the name of Jesus.

By the blood of Jesus, I destroy every familiar spirit caging my life and career.

Fire of God arrest every demonic agents, assigned to police my destiny and marriage.

By the blood of Jesus, I proclaim no weapon fashioned against me shall ever prosper.

Holy Spirit of God break me through and forward in life in the mighty name of Jesus.

God, smash me and renew my strength, in the name of Jesus.

Holy Spirit, open my eyes to see beyond the visible to the invisible, in the name of Jesus.

Father Lord grant me strength and power in the name of Jesus

O Lord, liberate my spirit to follow the leading of the Holy Spirit.

Holy Spirit, teach me to pray through problems instead of praying about, it in the name of Jesus.

Father Lord, deliver me from the false accusation in life, in the name of Jesus

By the blood of Jesus, every evil spiritual padlock and evil chain hindering my success, be roasted, in the name of Jesus.

By the blood of Jesus I rebuke every spirit of spiritual deafness and blindness in my life, in the name of Jesus.

Father Lord, empower me to dominate the enemy of my destiny in the name of Jesus.

Jesus Christ of Nazareth, heal my infirmities in the name of Jesus

Lord, anoint my eyes and my ears that they may see and hear wonderous things from heaven.

Father Lord, anoint me with power and authority to dominate all my enemies in the name of Jesus.

Fire of God roast every giant rising up against my life and career.

Holy Spirit of God destroy all my oppressors in the name of Jesus.

Angels of good new, bring my good news to me in the mighty name of Jesus.

Every strong man holding me down, lose your hold now in the name of Jesus.

I nullify every demonic prediction over my life in the name of Jesus.

By the blood of Jesus, I flush out every polluted deposit of the enemy in my life.

By the blood of Jesus, I paralyze every enemy of my promotion in the name of Jesus.

Father Lord, destroy any power tormenting my life that is not from you.
Holy Ghost fire, ignite the fire of revival in my life.

By the blood of Jesus, I declare victory over every conflicting trial.

By the Blood of Jesus, I command the arrest of every demonic spirit, militating against my life

By the blood of Jesus, I proclaimed the blood of Jesus, over every device of the enemy.

By the blood of Jesus, I revoke stagnation and hardship over my life in the name of Jesus.

Holy Ghost fire, destroy every satanic arrangement in my life, in the name of Jesus.

By the Blood of Jesus, I command the arrest of every demonic spirit, militating against my life

By the blood of Jesus, I proclaimed the blood of Jesus, over every device of the enemy.

By the blood of Jesus, I revoke stagnation and hardship over my life in the name of Jesus.

Holy Ghost fire, destroy every satanic arrangement in my life, in the name of Jesus.

# Prayer point for protection

- It is written, *"Do not be afraid of sudden terror; nor of the trouble from the wicked when it comes; for the Lord will be your confidence. And will keep your foot from being caught."* **(Proverb 3:26).**

- Therefore, O Lord, cover us and our loved ones from the activities of terrorists, in Jesus name!

- It is written, *"avenge me of my adversary"* **(Luke. 18:3).**

- Therefore, O Lord, arise and avenge us of all my adversaries in the name of Jesus!

- It is written, *"They fought from the heavens; the stars from their courses fought against Sisera"* **(Judges. 5:20).**

- Therefore O heavens, fight for us in Jesus name!

- It is written, *"I will purge the rebels from among you, and those who transgress against Me; I will bring them out of the country where they dwell, but they shall not enter the land of Israel. They will know that I am the Lord"* **(Ezekiel. 20:38)**

- Therefore, O Lord, purge and sanitize our household in the name of Jesus!

- It is written, *"Then it was so, after all your wickedness – "woe, woe to you!" says the Lord God"* **(Ezekiel. 16:23)**

- Therefore, woe unto all the vessels that the enemy is using to do us harm in the name of Jesus!

- It is written, *"Behold therefore, I stretch out My hand against you, admonished your allotment, and gave you up to the will of those who hate you..."* **(Ezek. 16:27)**

- Therefore, let our enemies be delivered into the hands of their enemies in Jesus name!

- It is written, *"You shall be for fuel of fire; your blood shall be in the midst of the land. You shall not be remembered, for I the Lord have spoken"* **(Ezekiel. 21:32)**

- Therefore, let all our spiritual enemies become fuel for divine fire in Jesus name!

- It is written, *"Then they will know that I am the Lord, when I have set a fire in Egypt and all her helpers are destroyed"* **(Ezekiel. 30:8).**

- Therefore, O Lord, let all the helpers of our enemies be destroyed in the name of Jesus.

- It is written, *"And the people to whom they prophesy shall be cast out in the streets of Jerusalem because of the famine and the sword; they will have no one to bury them – them nor their wives, their sons nor their daughters – for I will pour their wickedness on them"* **(Jer. 14:16).**

- Therefore, O Lord, pour the wickedness of those who seek to destroy us upon their own heads in the name of Jesus!

- It is written, *"Call together the archers against Babylon. All you who bend the bow encamp against it all around; let none of them escape. Repay her according to her work; According to all she has done, do to her; for she has been poured against the Lord, against the Holy one of Israel"* **(Jer. 50:29).**

- Therefore, let all the hosts of the Lord turn against our spiritual enemies in Jesus name!

- It is written, *"Let God arise, let His enemies be scattered; let those also who hate him flee before him"* **(Psalms. 68:1).**

- Therefore, O God, arise and let all your enemies in our lives be scattered in Jesus name!

- It is written, *"And He that searches the hearts knows what the mind of the spirit is, because He makes intercession for the saints according to the will of God"* **(Romans 8:27)**

- Therefore, the intercessory prayers of Jesus, who is seated on the right hand of the throne of God, will not be in vain over our lives, in the name of Jesus.

- It is written, *"The Lord is your keeper; the Lord is the shade at your right hand. The sun shall not strike you by day, nor the moon by night. The Lord shall preserve you from all evil; He shall preserve your soul. The Lord shall preserve your going out and your coming in from this time forth, and even forevermore"* **(Psalms. 121:5-8)**

- Therefore, O Lord, spread your covering of fire and the blood of Jesus over us and our loved ones, in the name of Jesus.

- It is written, *"Rejoice always, pray without ceasing, in everything give thanks; for this is the will of God in Christ Jesus for you" (1 Thess. 5:16:18).*

- Therefore, we thank you Father, for raising a spiritual shield over our loved ones and us. Thank you for giving us the heart for appreciating everything you are doing for us. Thank you for filling our hearts and our home with joy and peace that surpasses all understanding. Blessed be your name for all the answers to our prayers in the name of Jesus!

- You are holy, holy, Lord God Almighty, who was and is and is to come, Amen!

- O Lord, let our season of divine intervention appear in the name of Jesus!

- O you gates in the heavenlies standing against our destiny, lift up your heads in the name of Jesus!

- O you gates in the waters standing against our destiny, lift up your heads in the name of Jesus!

- O you gates in the earth standing against our destiny, lift up your heads in the name of Jesus!

- O you gates under the earth standing against our destiny, lift up your heads in the name of Jesus!

- O God, arise and destroy every gate keeper assigned against our lives in the name of Jesus!

- We break the backbone of every spirit of scarcity in our lives in the name of Jesus!

- O Lord anoint our eyes to see divine opportunities in the name of Jesus!

- Lord let every blindness to the treasures of our lives be cleared in the name of Jesus!

- Let our divine helpers appear in the name of Jesus!

- We declare, O Lord, that the rest of our lives will be better than the first part, in Jesus name!

- We declare, O Lord that will overcome obstacles and defeat every enemy, in Jesus name!

- We declare, O Lord that every blessing and promise that you put in our hearts will come to pass because this is our time for favour, in Jesus name!

- We declare, O Lord that this is a new season of increase in our lives. We speak health, wisdom, creativity, divine connections and supernatural opportunities. They are coming our way, in Jesus name!

- We declare, O Lord that we choose faith over fear. We are victorious in faith, in Jesus name!

- We declare, O Lord that that we are not just surviving, this is our time to thrive in prosperity, in Jesus name!

- We declare, O Lord that we will believe that we have received in the spirit even though we do not see anything happening in the flesh, in Jesus name!

- We declare, O Lord that our rewards are being transferred to us because we remain in faith, in Jesus name!

- We declare, O Lord that doubt will not ruin our optimistic spirit, in Jesus name!

- We declare, O Lord that we are prisoners of hope and get up every morning expecting your favour, in Jesus name!

- We declare, O Lord that you will do amazing things in our lives, in Jesus name!

- We declare, O Lord that we are closer to your abundant blessing than we think, our time has come, your promises will come to pass, in Jesus name!

- We declare, O Lord that we will stay in an attitude of faith and expectation, in Jesus name!

- We declare, O Lord that we are not worried, we know that you are our vindicator. It may seem to be taking a long time, but we will reap in due season if trust in you Lord, in Jesus name!

- We declare, O Lord that you know the secret petitions our heart and we believe that they will come to fulfilment, in Jesus name!

- We declare, O Lord that you will open new doors for us, in Jesus name!

- We declare, O Lord that we will see your goodness, in Jesus name!

- We declare, O Lord that this is our time to believe because favour is coming our way, in Jesus name!

- We declare, O Lord that you have paved the way to abundant prosperity for us, prosperity more than we can every dream of or imagine, for your sake, in Jesus name!

- We declare, O Lord that in your eyes our future is extremely bright, in Jesus name!

- We declare, O Lord that we will rise higher and higher and see more of your favour and blessings and we will live the prosperous life you have in store for us, in Jesus name!

- We declare, O Lord that we may have a lot of turmoil, but we know that everything is going to be alright, in Jesus name!

- We declare, O Lord that we may have a lot of turmoil, but we know that everything is going to be alright, in Jesus name!

- We declare, O Lord that we have faith because we have put you first, in Jesus name!

- We thank you, O Lord that our set time for favour is here, in Jesus name!

- We declare, O Lord that our hour of deliverance has come, in Jesus name!

- We declare, O Lord that there is no limit to what we can do, in Jesus name!

- We declare, O Lord that there is no obstacle we cannot overcome, in Jesus name!

- We declare, O Lord that that we have seen your accomplishments and they are good, in Jesus name!

- We declare, O Lord that there is no challenge that is too great for us because you are with us, in Jesus name!

- We declare, O Lord that you always succeed, in Jesus name!

- We declare, O Lord that there is no financial difficulty or situation in our lives that is too great for you to resolve, in Jesus name!

- We declare, O Lord that you are our Father Jehovah Jireh and that you own everything and you are our provider, in Jesus name!

- We declare, O Lord that your promises declare that we are destined to live a victorious life, in Jesus name!

- We declare, O Lord that we are your children, in Jesus name!

- We declare, O Lord that the seeds of increase, success and promotion are taking a new root; your favour will spring forth in our lives in a great way; we will see new seasons of blessings and new seasons of your favour. It's our time to have abundant faith, in Jesus name!

- O Lord, it is written; according to your faith, it will be done unto you. Ps. 2:8 says "ask me and I will give you the nations as your inheritance."

- Therefore, we ask you Lord to fulfil our highest hopes and dreams, in Jesus name!

- We ask you this day, O Lord to give us our abundant blessing now, in Jesus name!

- We dare to exercise our faith by asking you O Lord so that we may receive indeed, in Jesus name!

- We thank you O Lord that for encouraging our faith, in Jesus name!

- We declare, O Lord that this is our time for favour, in Jesus name!

- We declare, O Lord that this is our time to prosper abundantly, in Jesus name!

- We declare, O Lord that this is our time to have instant answers to prayer, in Jesus name!

- We declare, O Lord that this is our time to ask and receive, in Jesus name!

- We declare, O Lord that this is our time to thank you and testify for answered prayer, in Jesus name!

- We declare, O Lord that we are blessed and that goodness and mercy are following us right now, in Jesus name!

- We declare, O Lord that you favor is surrounding us like a shield – you prosper us even in the desert, in Jesus name!

- We declare, O Lord that you have great things for us in the spirit and that you have already released favor into our prayers, in Jesus name!

- We declare, O Lord that you are a great and Holy God, in Jesus name!

- It is written, *"Delight yourself in the Lord and he will give you the desires of your heart"* **(Ps 37:4).**

- We therefore declare, O Lord that we delight in you because you are our Father God and because we are your children you have made us the head and not the tail.

- We declare, O Lord that because we are your children, we are more than conquerors, in Jesus name!

- We declare, O Lord that we are blessed and you supply all our needs. We have more than enough, in Jesus name!

- We declare, O Lord that we have abundant favor indeed, in Jesus name!

- We declare, O Lord that we are filled indeed with the presence of the Holy Spirit, in Jesus name!

- We declare, O Lord that we have abundant faith indeed, in Jesus name!

- We declare, O Lord that you have answered our prayers, in Jesus name!

- We declare, O Lord that our debts are all paid up, in Jesus name!

- We declare, O Lord that we are healthy, in Jesus name!

- We declare, O Lord that we have no lack and that we have more than enough, in Jesus name!

- We declare, O Lord that we are extremely blessed so much that we can bless your kingdom, in Jesus name!

- We declare, O Lord that we are extremely blessed so much that we can bless others, in Jesus name!

- We declare, O Lord that we have entered into an anointing of ease, in Jesus name!

- We declare, O Lord that for every opportunity we have missed, every chance we've blown, you will turn the clock and bring bigger and better things across our path, in Jesus name!

- We declare, O Lord that we will not settle for less than your best, in Jesus name!

- Please restore the time that we have lost, O Lord that, in Jesus name!

- Restore our victories, O Lord, in Jesus name!

- Restore our lost joy, lost peace, lost health, lost insight, lost faith, lost dedication, and desire to please you, we declare, O Lord in Jesus name!

- We declare, O Lord that you use what was meant for our harm to our advantage, in Jesus name!

- We declare, O Lord that you are a faithful God, in Jesus name!

- We declare, O Lord that you will blossom our lives in ways that we can never imagine, in Jesus name!

- We know, O Lord that you will bless us abundantly, in Jesus name!

- We know, O Lord that you will provide divine connections, in Jesus name!

- We declare, O Lord that we are not suffering – we are blessed, in Jesus name!

- We declare, O Lord that our difficulties will give way to new growth, new opportunities, and new vision, in Jesus name!

- O Lord let us see your blessing bloom in our lives in ways we would never dreamt possible, in Jesus name!

- We declare, O Lord that we will stay in faith, so that what was meant to stop us will not be a stumbling block but a stepping stone taking us to a higher level, in Jesus name!

- We declare, O Lord that we are not ordinary, but we are children of the most high God, in Jesus name!

- We declare, O Lord that we created to rise above problems, in Jesus name!

- We declare victory over strife O Lord, in Jesus name!

- We declare, O Lord that no weapon formed against us shall prosper, in Jesus name!

- We declare, O Lord that we are healthy and that no sickness shall live in us, in Jesus name!

- We declare, O Lord that triumph is our birthright, in Jesus name!

- We declare, O Lord that our setbacks are simply setups for greater comebacks that will place us to be better than we were before, in Jesus name!

- We declare, O Lord that with you all things are possible, in Jesus name!

- We declare, O Lord that we are in agreement with you. We know you have supernatural favour in store for us. You have supernatural opportunities, supernatural healing and supernatural restoration, in Jesus name!

- We declare, O Lord that you want to do unusual things in our lives, in Jesus name!

- We declare, O Lord that in faith, we have expectation deep in our spirits, in Jesus name!

- We declare, O Lord that this will not be a survival year but a supernatural year in which you will abundantly come through for us, in Jesus name!

- We believe, O Lord that you have come through for us, in Jesus name!

- We declare, O Lord that because we hope in you, we will not be put to shame, in Jesus name!

- We declare, O Lord that your word is right and true, you are faithful in all you do, in Jesus name!

- We declare, O Lord that you are our refuge and strength, an ever present helper, in Jesus name!

- We declare, O Lord that we will cast our cares on you and you will sustain us, you will never let the righteous fall, in Jesus name!

- We declare, O Lord that you are the strength of our hearts and our portion forever, in Jesus name!

- We declare, O Lord that you are our dwelling, therefore, no harm will befall us and no disaster will come near our tent, in Jesus name!

- We declare, O Lord that you are our refuge and our fortress, in Jesus name!

- We declare, O Lord that you will command your angels concerning us to guard us in all our ways, in Jesus name!

- We declare, O Lord that even in darkness the light will dawn for us, in Jesus name!

- We declare, O Lord that your word is eternal and stands firm in the heavens, in Jesus name!

- We declare, O Lord that your faithfulness will continue throughout all generations, in Jesus name!

- We declare, O Lord that you will keep us from harm; you will watch over our lives; you will watch over our coming and our going both now and for evermore, in Jesus name! **(Ps. 121)**

- Thank you O Lord for the assurance that you are watching over us even when we sleep, in Jesus name! **(Ps. 13:5-6)**

- We declare, O Lord that you will drive those that do evil away from us and that you will protect us from their influence, in Jesus name! **(Ps. 66:1-4)**

- We will shout with joy to you O Lord, we will sing the glory of your name and make your praise glorious. How awesome are your deeds! So great is your power that your enemies cringe before you, in Jesus name!

- We declare, O Lord that that we will give you thanks for you answered us, in Jesus name! **(Ps. 118:21)**

- We declare, O Lord that we will praise you with all our hearts; before the gods we will sing your praise. We will bow down towards your Holy temple and will praise your name for your love and your faithfulness, for you have exalted above all things, your name and your word, in Jesus name! **(Ps. 138:1-3) Amen!**

## WHY DON'T WE GIVE TO GOD AND TO THE POOR?

Most good people do not give money to anyone because they lack the understanding. Really, it is not that they are selfish, but because they lack the insight, and the understanding to give to God.

We are told… *"He that hath pity upon the poor lendeth unto the Lord; and that which he hath given will he pay him again."* **Proverb 19:17.**

This short story will interest you. A fellow gave into our prayer ministry online and few weeks down the line, he requested for his money back. Every time you think you gave to a man, or a pastor, you just wasted your money away. If you must give to God, then you must get the revelation of the word of God.

It is written *"He that giveth unto the poor shall not lack: but he that hideth his eyes shall have many a curse."* **Proverb28:27**

Although Jesus commanded us to "give and it shall be given unto us" studies have suggested that an average Christian does not give freely-and willingly. We are told that God loves a cheerful giver. But how many of us can testify to cheerful giving?

**-We do not give, because we do not believe**

It is written *"But as many as received him, to them gave he power to become the sons of God, even to them that believe on his name."*

Unbelief is a stigma that hinders us from Giving & Receiving from God. As long as you do not believe in giving, you are not entitled to receive anything from the Lord.

It is written *"John answered and said, A man can receive nothing, except it be given him from heaven."* **John 3:27.**

Jesus said *"I am the vine, ye are the branches: He that abideth in me, and I in him, the same bringeth forth much fruit: for without me ye can do nothing."* **John 15:5**

**~We do not give because of our selfish character**

For the most part, most non givers are people who have made selfishness a life style.

For the most part, selfish people are reduced to self, while givers live forever. Do you remember JC Penny and John D Rockefeller? These are men that their legacy will forever live.

Why? Simply because they gave beyond their power. (more than enough in their life time).

It is written, *"Be not deceived; God is not mocked: for whatsoever a man soweth, that shall he also reap. For he that soweth to his flesh shall of the flesh reap corruption; but he that soweth to the Spirit shall of the Spirit reap life everlasting. And let us not be weary in well doing: for in due season we shall reap, if we faint not."*

Selfishness is a weakness of the flesh. *"For to be carnally minded is death; but to be spiritually minded is life and peace. Because the carnal mind is enmity against God: for it is not subject to the law of God, neither indeed can be. So then they that are in the flesh cannot please God."* **(Romans 8:6-8)**

### ~We do not receive because we give grudgingly

It is written, *"But this I say, He which soweth sparingly shall reap also sparingly; and he which soweth bountifully shall reap also bountifully. Every man according as he purposeth in his heart, so let him give; not grudgingly, or of necessity: for God loveth a cheerful giver. Every time we are giving to God, we must be excited about it otherwise we miss our harvest."*

*"He that giveth unto the poor shall not lack: but he that hideth his eyes shall have many a curse."* **Proverb 28:27**

*"He that hath pity upon the poor lendeth unto the Lord; and that which he hath given will he pay him again."* **Proverb 19:17**

*"Cast thy bread upon the waters: for thou shalt find it after many days."* **Eccl 11:1**

*"Give a portion to seven, and also to eight; for thou knowest not what evil shall be upon the earth."* **Eccl 11:2**

*"Blessed is he that considereth the poor: the Lord will deliver him in time of trouble."* **Isaiah41:1**

If you must come out of sickness, you must embrace giving as a lifestyle. If the elephant was to retain all that He/she eats, he will die by eating. There are so many greedy men and women who have more than enough. If you must live long embrace giving to your local church, to your pastor and to the poor, the orphans, and the helpless.

*"The Lord will preserve him, and keep him alive; and he shall be blessed upon the earth: and thou wilt not deliver him unto the will of his enemies."* **Isaiah41:2**

*"The Lord will strengthen him upon the bed of languishing: thou wilt make all his bed in his sickness."* **Isaiah41:3**

# CHAPTER 1
## The Grace to Give

*"Moreover, brethren, we do you to wit of the grace of God bestowed on the churches of Macedonia; How that in a great trial of affliction the abundance of their joy and their deep poverty abounded unto the riches of their liberality. For to their power, I bear record, yea, and beyond their power they were willing of themselves."* **2cor8:1-3**

It takes the Grace of God to give a penny to any congregation. To me, giving includes our time for prayer, worship, and praise. Every dedicated church worker have a great reward from our heavenly Father. If you do not pray for your local congregation, who do you expect to pray for them?

If you do not support your local church and pastor, who do you expect to support them? *We are told by the Holy Scriptures, for God so love He gave. If we claim we love God, we must embrace giving to God as a lifestyle.*

It is written *"For God so loved the world that he gave his only begotten Son, that whosoever believeth in him should not perish, but have everlasting life."* **John 3:16.**

*"We know that we have passed from death unto life, because we love the brethren. He that loveth not his brother abideth in death."* **1John 3:14**

*"And we have known and believed the love that God hath to us. God is love; and he that dwelleth in love dwelleth in God, and God in him."* **1John 4:16**

## THE "LOVE OF GOD" IS OUR PRIMARY REASON TO GIVE

It is written *"By this we know that we love the children of God, when we love God, and keep his commandments. For this is the love of God, that we keep his commandments: and his commandments are not grievous."* **1John 5:2-3**

## Chapter 1 - The Grace to Give

Giving to the less privilege, to your local church assembly and to your local pastor is the commandment of God. It will interest you to know that one of the greatest secret of the richest man that ever lived was that he was a giver. King Solomon gave so much that he made headline news in those days in the bible.

*"And Solomon loved the Lord, walking in the statutes of David his father: only he sacrificed and burnt incense in high places. And the king went to Gibeon to sacrifice there; for that was the great high place: a thousand burnt offerings did Solomon offer upon that altar."* **1king3:3-4**

We must always *give out of our love* for Jesus Christ, and the kingdom of God. We must always give because we love our pastor. It takes the grace of God and faith to sow a seed into the kingdom of God. Remember Jesus brought us grace and truth.

The word of God says, *"And of his fulness have all we received, and grace for grace. For the law was given by Moses, but grace and truth came by Jesus Christ."* **John1:16-17**

The Law of Giving and Receiving by Franklin N. Abazie

It is written *"Cast thy bread upon the waters: for thou shalt find it after many days."* The preacher said *"Give a portion to seven, and also to eight; for thou knowest not what evil shall be upon the earth."*

God takes pleasure whenever we give in faith.

We must embrace the giving grace of God. One thing I love for you to know, is that it is a principle. If you give, you shall reap.

There are no two ways about it. *"While the earth remaineth, seedtime and harvest, and cold and heat, and summer and winter, and day and night shall not cease."*

Some of our active parishioners give all the time. That is why God keep blessing them every time. Other stingy *members never give*.

Those *who never give in life*, always celebrate lack in their lives. But I thank God that as small as our ministry is, God is sending us the supply per day as we move forward as a prayer ministry.

## Chapter 1 - The Grace to Give

Most ministries that are reluctant to ask believers for donations, however, will suffer stagnation, and fall far short of its potential for the Kingdom of God.

The best approach to ministry, calls for a gracious balance between giving and receiving: This I mean-making the needs of the ministry known and being content to wait on the Lord to supply our true needs according to His riches. **Philippians 4:10-19.**

As a minister, never feel ashamed, or embarrassed to ask for donations and financial support. It is written *"Ask, and it shall be given you; seek, and ye shall find; knock, and it shall be opened unto you"* **Mathew 7:7.**

If you do not ask, you will never receive. *"For every one that asketh receiveth; and he that seeketh findeth; and to him that knocketh it shall be opened."* **Mathew 7:8**

As long as we are truly doing God's work, God will supply all our needs. As believers, our greatest hindrance from giving to any Christian ministry is confidence, trust, love, faith, and miracles.

Often some folks want me to prophecy into their life before they can give into our ministry. This thing does not work this way. If you honor me as a prophet of God, God will reward you with supernatural blessing.

A man of God said and I quote *"Your reaction to your pastor determines God's reaction to your life."*

It is important to note that how we handle our finances is important to God. It reflects where our hearts and priorities.

It is written *"Wherefore the Lord said, Forasmuch as this people draw near me with their mouth, and with their lips do honour me, but have removed their heart far from me, and their fear toward me is taught by the precept of men:"* **Isaiah 29:13**

## Chapter 1 - The Grace to Give

It is written *"Honour the Lord with thy substance, and with the first fruits of all thine increase: So shall thy barns be filled with plenty, and thy presses shall burst out with new wine."* **Proverb3:9-10**

First of all, giving to God should be out of our love for God. *"For God so loved the world that he gave his only begotten Son, that whosoever believeth in him should not perish, but have everlasting life."* **John3:16**

Secondly giving to God should be cheerfully and willingly. *"But this I say, He which soweth sparingly shall reap also sparingly; and he which soweth bountifully shall reap also bountifully. Every man according as he purposeth in his heart, so let him give; not grudgingly, or of necessity: for God loveth a cheerful giver."* **2cor9:6-7**

Thirdly, giving to God should be freely and willingly. Jesus said "Freely you received, freely give." To give freely means give not expecting or even desiring some temporal personal benefit in return. All that we have is from God, and He commands us to give freely.

We ought not to expect something in return as if we are looking for approval or honor before men, but simply because we have the privilege of being able to give. Just like I say all the time, giving is a privilege, it is part of the commandment.

It is written *"For this is the love of God, that we keep his commandments: and his commandments are not grievous."* **1John5:3**

Fourthly, we must give our best and not left over. *"Noah builded an altar unto the Lord; and took of every clean beast, and of every clean fowl, and offered burnt offerings on the altar."*

A lot of people love to give God left over. God is not in need and will never be in need.

We are told *"Ye offer polluted bread upon mine altar; and ye say, Wherein have we polluted thee? In that ye say, The table of the Lord is contemptible . And if ye offer the*

## Chapter 1 - The Grace to Give

*blind for sacrifice, is it not evil? and if ye offer the lame and sick, is it not evil? offer it now unto thy governor; will he be pleased with thee, or accept thy person? saith the Lord of hosts."* **Malachi 1:7-8**

Fifthly, we must give in secret and humbly. Some people want everybody to know that they just purchased an altar stand for the church. Whenever you do such, you steal the glory of God.

*"But when you give to the poor, do not let your left hand know what your right hand is doing, so that your giving will be in secret; and your Father who sees what is done in secret will reward you."* We will have had our reward in full if we are seeking to give for the sake of looking good to others.

Those who give to be seen by men have forfeited their eternal reward and their joy in exchange for temporal recognition and renown by mere people. Giving in secret keeps others from having a chance to judge us, envy us, compare with us, or applaud us.

Churches need to be mindful of their times of taking in financial gifts that the system does not contribute to judgment, ranking, competition, etc. Others have no business knowing what we give as a family unit to Christ's work and church, and we have a responsibility not to showcase or flaunt what we give.

Neither should we feel embarrassed or worry about being put to shame. There are few joys on earth as being able to freely give to others without anybody else knowing.

Sixthly, we are to give according to our ability. *"Every man according as he purposeth in his heart"* We can't give what we don't have, and we are not to put our families at risk of not having a home to live in or food to eat.

God understands the high cost of living. We must meet our debts and expenses so as to keep a good testimony before men. What good does it do to give to a charity and then fail to pay a bill or bounce a check?

## Chapter 1 - The Grace to Give

We do more good for the kingdom by living in balance and following God's leading per time.

There are times that God will move us to give above what we feel able to do **(2 Corinthians 8:3).**

There are times God will test our faith by our giving ability. Often, God will call us to give in such a way that really requires faith from our heart. This is one of God's ways to cause us to experience growth in Christ through an increasing need to rely upon Him in faith.

If this is the case, God will make it clear. We are instructed to give in faith. The word says, *"Cast thy bread upon the waters: for thou shalt find it after many days. Give a portion to seven, and also to eight; for thou knowest not what evil shall be upon the earth."* **Eccl11:1-2**

Seventhly, we will reap in proportion to that which we sow. 2 Corinthians 9:6 says, *"Now this I say, he who sows sparingly will also reap sparingly, and he who sows bountifully will also reap bountifully."*

In other words, those who give generously will themselves be given back to generously by God. No one can say exactly how God will repay a person's generosity or exactly when it will happen, so we must beware of any who claim to know the mind of God in regard to our finances.

God honors those who give to His work bountifully, abundantly, and generously. Generosity within our ability is a sacrifice that leads to great joy and reward.

Eighthly, we are not to give out of duty and against our free-will but cheerfully and willingly. 2 Corinthians 9:7 says that our giving is not to be done *"grudgingly or under compulsion, for God loves a cheerful giver."* God wants giving to be a happy experience, not a drudgery or mere requirement.

## Chapter 1 - The Grace to Give

The giver is not trying to satisfy the harsh expectations of a deity, nor is he supposed to be giving begrudgingly and against his will. Giving is a "want to" thing.

What we are saying here is that God is a loving father and not a wicked judge. There is no portion of the scripture that says if you do not give, you will go to hell. The same principle applies to tithing also. And in fact all kinds of charity donations.

God moves in a person to give joyfully and cheerfully. The word for cheerful could also mean "prompt or ready to act." In other words, a cheerful giver is both a joyful giver and an eager giver, ready, willing, desiring, and prepared to give.

Ninthly, we give as the Lord leads us individually. 2 Corinthians 9:7 says, *"Each one must do just as he has purposed in his heart."* We are not to give because our pastor motivated us by giving us a guilt trip about tithing.

We are not to give so that we can get God off our backs or to earn His favor. Rather, we are to give because we want to give and because we believe that God would be honored by our giving. If we are not purposing in our hearts to give or if we find that we have no desire to give, we had better ask the Lord why these things are the case.

It is one thing to be unsure about a church or a ministry and be hesitant to give to it. It is another thing to be hesitant to give altogether. The important thing is that we are faithful and willing to give where and to the extent that God leads us to give.

Giving is an indescribable gift in and of itself (2 Corinthians 9:15). The world cannot understand this as they do not enjoy giving for the most part; they enjoy getting. The Christian's way is backwards, getting much more joy out of giving than receiving.

Jesus Himself said, *"It is more blessed to give than to receive"* **(Acts 20:35).** Thus, in giving we truly receive.

## Chapter 1 - The Grace to Give

*"The liberal soul shall be made fat: and he that watereth shall be watered also himself."* **Prover11:25**

Abraham became very rich even in His old age because he was a great giver. It is written *"And Abraham was old, and well stricken in age: and the Lord had blessed Abraham in all things."* **Genesis24:1**

### Who should give?

As long as we desire to prosper and to live, we must embrace this teaching on giving and receiving. Everyone who desire to prosper in life should give to the Lord. Giving should become a burden to anyone.

*" Let everyone lay by him in store, as God has prospered him."* **1cor 16:2**

### Why should we give?

1) We should give to command supernatural increase in our lives.

2) We should give to live, and for protection.

3) We should give because all the tithe belong to the Lord.

4) We should give out of our Love for God. **1king3:3, John3:16**

5) We should give out of a liberal heart. **Proverb11:25**

6) We should give cheerfully. **2cor9:7**

7) We should give out of a willingly heart. **1cor9:17, exodus35:5-22**

8) We should give to live and to be healthy **Psalm41:1-3**

9) We should give to seek the kingdom of God. **Mathew.6:33**

10) We should give in faith. **Eccl11:1**

11) We should give our best not left over. **Malachi1:6-8, 2sam24:24**

12) We should give in righteousness. **Malachi3:3**

13) We should give our best and not left overs. **(genesis8:20-21, Mal1:6-8)**

# CHAPTER 2
## The Power to Receive

*"He came unto his own, and his own received him not. But as many as received him, to them gave he power to become the sons of God, even to them that believe on his name"*
**John 1:11-12**

We are told *"But ye shall receive power, after that the Holy Ghost is come upon you: and ye shall be witnesses unto me both in Jerusalem, and in all Judaea, and in Samaria, and unto the uttermost part of the earth."* **Acts 1:8.**

If you do what guarantees His Presence and Power, it will automatically flow into your life.

Listen to this *"And, behold, I send the promise of my Father upon you: but tarry ye in the city of Jerusalem, until ye be endued with power from on high."* **Luke 24:49.**

Like I said in the opening scriptures, giving and receiving is a law. It is like the laws of gravity. If you do not sow, you will never reap. As simple as that.

It is written *"While the earth remaineth, seedtime and harvest, and cold and heat, and summer and winter, and day and night shall not cease."* **Genesis 8:22**

So many of us lack the grace to receive from God. It takes the Grace of God to receive anything from anyone. Some folks will never be able to receive anything in their life time because they lack the anointing to receive.

As long as we neglect that Power to receive, we will never receive from any source.

Few months ago, a man walked up to me in New York City, and within a five minute conversation, He gave me $500.00 for speaking into His life. I pray you covet such grace in your life in Jesus Mighty Name.

## Chapter 2 - The Power to Receive

There are some strange receiving power that God has given to me as a man of God. I indulge you to crave and be part of it in the Name of Jesus.

## What will you love to receive from the Lord?

*"My sheep hear my voice, and I know them, and they follow me"*
**John 10:27**

We must hear His voice. The act of sowing and reaping is a universal law. If we must receive we must embrace the act of giving to others. The power to receive is hidden in our heart. I wonder how some people think?

The bible says that *"The heart is deceitful above all things, and desperately wicked: who can know it?"* **Jer 17:9**

The churches of Macedonia received so much from Apostle Paul simply because they understood the principles of receiving.

Talking about them the Holy bible said that despite their afflictions, they were willing of themselves to give to Apostle Paul.

## The Macedonia church

*"How that in a great trial of affliction the abundance of their joy and their deep poverty abounded unto the riches of their liberality."* 2cor8:2

*"For to their power, I bear record, yea, and beyond their power they were willing of themselves"* **2cor8:3**

I will challenge you to start giving upward and watch your life take a new turn. The reason for all the affliction and hardship is because we are very selfish. The bible said that *"The liberal soul shall be made fat: and he that watereth shall be watered also himself."* **Proverb 11:25**

*"And my God will meet all your needs according to his glorious riches in Christ Jesus."* **Philippians 4:19**

## Chapter 2 - The Power to Receive

We must embrace living our life by faith, and depending on God. Whenever you trust God, your supply is unstoppable. Simply because our supply is from the Lord.

*"Bring the whole tithe into the storehouse, that there may be food in my house. Test me in this,' says the LORD Almighty, "and see if I will not throw open the floodgates of heaven and pour out so much blessing that you will not have room enough for it."* **Malachi 3:10**

It is a bold step of faith to start tithing. Some cynics contest the act of tithing in the New Testament. Although I agree to a degree, for our salvation is no longer based on works, but on faith in Jesus. But the truth is, as a New Testament believers, ten percent should just be a yardstick to measure our giving ability.

After all, God owns it all and no matter where we are as far as what we are giving, we should always be striving to give more.

*"And all the tithe of the land, whether of the seed of the land, or of the fruit of the tree, is the Lord's: it is holy unto the Lord."* **Leviticus 27:30**

Like I always say, without the revelation of the knowledge of God, none of us will be able to receive from the Holy Spirit. It takes an insight to receive anything from God. If you must receive, you must give liberally to God others.

*"But ye shall receive power, after that the Holy Ghost is come upon you: and ye shall be witnesses unto me both in Jerusalem, and in all Judaea, and in Samaria, and unto the uttermost part of the earth."* **Acts 1:8**

Consider the conditions and benefits of God's promises as identified in the following Scriptures from the Amplified Bible:

## Chapter 2 - The Power to Receive

**Psalm 35:27:**

*"Let those who favor my righteous cause, and have pleasure in my uprightness shout for joy and be glad and say continuously, Let the Lord be magnified, Who takes pleasure in the prosperity of His servant."*

**Psalm 84:11:**

*"For the Lord God is a Sun and Shield; the Lord bestows [present] grace and favor and [future] glory (honor, splendor, and heavenly bliss)! No good thing will He withhold from those who walk uprightly."*

**John 10:10:**

*"The thief comes in only in order to steal and kill and destroy. I came that they may have and enjoy life and have it in abundance (to the fill, till it overflows)."*

## 2 Corinthians 8:9:

*"For you are becoming progressively acquainted with and recognizing more strongly and clearly the grace of our Lord Jesus Christ (His kindness, His gracious generosity, His undeserved favor and spiritual blessing), [in] that though He was [so very] rich, yet for your sakes He became [so very] poor, in order that by His poverty you might become enriched (abundantly supplied)."*

## Deuteronomy 8:18:

*"But you shall [earnestly] remember the Lord your God, for it is He Who gives you power to get wealth, that He may establish His covenant which He swore to your fathers, as it is this day."*

## Proverbs 3:9-10:

*"Honor the Lord with your capital and sufficiency [from righteous labors] and with the first fruits of all your income; So shall your storage places be filled with plenty, and your vats shall be overflowing with new wine."*

## Chapter 2 - The Power to Receive

**Malachi 3:10:**

*"Bring all the tithes (the whole tenth of your income) into the storehouse, that there may be food in My house, and prove Me now by it, says the Lord of hosts, if I will not open the windows of heaven for you and pour you out a blessing, that there shall not be room enough to receive it."*

**Proverbs 19:17:**

*"He who has pity on the poor, lends to the Lord, and that which he has given He will repay to him."*

**James 1:27:**

*"External religious worship [religion as it is expressed in outward acts] that is pure and unblemished in the sight of God the Father is this: to visit and help and care for the orphans and widows in their affliction and need, and to keep oneself unspotted and uncontaminated from the world."*

## Exodus 22:22-24:

*"Ye shall not afflict any widow, or fatherless child. If you afflict them in any way, and they cry at all to Me, I will surely hear their cry. And My wrath shall burn; I will kill you with the sword, and your wives shall be widows, and your children fatherless."*

## Deuteronomy 28:10-13:

*"And all people of the earth shall see that you are called by the name [and in the presence of] the Lord, and they shall be afraid of you. And the Lord shall make you have a surplus of prosperity, through the fruit of your body, of your livestock, and of your ground, in the land which the Lord swore to your fathers to give you. The Lord shall open to you His good treasury, the heavens, to give the rain of your land in its season and to bless all the work of your hands; and you shall lend to many nations, but you shall not borrow. And the Lord shall make you the head, and not the tail; and you shall be above only, and you shall not be beneath, if you heed the commandments of the Lord your God which I command you this day and are watchful to do them."*

Chapter 2 - The Power to Receive

# CONCLUSION

*"Give, and it shall be given unto you; good measure, pressed down, and shaken together, and running over, shall men give into your bosom. For with the same measure that ye mete withal it shall be measured to you again."* **Luke6:38**

*We must always give, to be given.* There is no other way around it. Stingy folks make me laugh, they did not sow, how do you want to reap a harvest, especially if you are convinced that you did not sow?

*"Therefore if any man be in Christ, he is a new creature: old things are passed away; behold, all things are become new."* **2cor5:17.**

As a new creature we must embrace the lifestyle of giving to the poor, to God to our pastor and to our families and love one. No one should be left out.

## Now repeat this prayer after me;

Say Lord Jesus, I accept you today, as my Lord and my savior, forgive me of my sins wash me with your blood. Right now, I believe, I am sanctified, I am save, I am free, I am free from the Power of sin to serve the Lord Jesus. Thank you Lord for saving me. Amen.

## Congratulations: YOU ARE NOW A BORN AGAIN CHRISTIAN

## What must I do to determine my divine visitation?

To determine divine visitation you must be born again. The word says as many as received him, to them gave He power to become the sons of God. Even to them that believe on his name.

To qualify for divine visitation do the following sincerely

## Chapter 2 - The Power to Receive

1) Acknowledge that you are a sinner and that He died for you. **Rom3:23**.

2) Repent of your sins. **Acts 3:19, Luke13:5, 2Peter3:9**

3) Believe in your heart that Jesus died for your sin. **Romans10:10**

4) Confess Jesus as the Lord over your life. **Romans10:10, Acts2:21**

### Now repeat this Prayer after me

Say Lord Jesus, give me the grace to give out of love. Empower me to become a great giver in your kingdom. I thank you for knowing you. Amen.

I adjure you to watch the Spirit of God bear witness with your Spirit confirming His word with signs following. The word says The Spirit itself beareth witness with our spirit, that we are the children of God.

Join a bible believing church or join us on our weekly and Sunday worship services at 343 Sanford Avenue Newark New Jersey 07106.

# WISDOM KEYS

Every Productive Society is a society heading to the top

Millions of Nigerians run away from Nigeria, very few Nigerians stay in Nigeria.

My decision to return Nigeria is the will of God for my life

My short coming in America after 18 years, trained me to be wise, to think, reflect and reason appropriately.

If you train your mind to reason it will train your hands to earn money.

It is absurd to use the money of the heathen to build the kingdom of the living God.

Every Ministry reveals its agenda and goal either at the beginning or at the end. Be careful of your life it is your first Ministry.

The average American mind is conditioned for a continual quest to get new things and (discard the former) and throw away old things.

## Chapter 2 - The Power to Receive

When I considered well, my BMW jeep became my initial deposit for the work of the ministry in Nigeria

Everyone is waiting for you to change your mind until you change your thinking nothing changes around you.

Multiple academic degrees in other discipline gave me the chance to think, reflect and reason

What so everyone are thinking and reflecting at the moment reveals you to the time and the now factor

All events and intents are the product of precise thought processes, accurate reason every event is designed for a designated timeline

Wisdom is your ability to think, to create and invent. If you can think wise enough you will come out of penury

The distance between you and success is your creative ability to think reason and reflect accurate.

Success is the result of hard work, commitment resolve and determination learning from past mistakes and failing.

If you organize your mind you have organized your life and destiny.

There is a thin line between success and failure. If you look above and beyond you are on your way to success.

Wealth is your ability to think, power is your ability to reason and success is your ability to be informed.

If you can make use of your mind by thinking and reasoning God will make use of your life and destiny.

Think and Be Great

Reflect, Reason, think and be great

Famous people are born of woman

## Chapter 2 - The Power to Receive

That you will make it is your intention; that you will survive is your resolve, that you will succeed with changes is your determination, personal efforts and hard work.

No man was born a failure. Lack of vision is the end product of failure.

Working with mental patients encourages and aspire me to be a productive observant and dedicated to my assignment.

Successful people are not magicians, it is the will power combined with hard work, and determination and a resolve to succeed that make them succeed.

In the unequivocal state of the mind, intention is not a location or a position it is the state of the mind.

So many people think that they think. The mind is used to think reflect and reason. You will remain blind with your eye open until you can see with your mind by thinking.

There is no favoritism in accurate and precise calculation

Although knowledge is power, information is the key and gateway to a great future.

It will take the hand of God to move the hand of man.

With the backing of the great wise God, nothing will disconnect you from your inheritance.

As long as you have wisdom and understanding of God, Satan and evil cannot manipulate your life and destiny.

You have come this far by yourself judgment and decision you have made in the past, now lean and listen to God for another dimension of greatness.

Great people are common people it is extra ordinary effort and the price of sacrifice that produces greatness.

As a mental direct care worker I saw a great pastor and a motivational speaker within myself.

Menial job does not reduce your self-worth, until you resolve to achieve greatness see greatness in all you do; you will never count in your community

## Chapter 2 - The Power to Receive

The principle of Jesus will solve your gambling and addiction problems

The man of Jesus will lead you into heaven,

Everyone have their self-appraisal and what they think about you. Until you discover yourself other opinion about you will alter the real you.

Supervisors and directors are just a position in the chain of command in a work place. Never allow your supervisor hierarchy to alter your opinion about yourself.

Everyone can come out of debt if they make up their mind.

That I am not a decision maker at work does not diminish my contribution to my world.

Although it appears like it was a poor decision to accept a direct care employment at a psychiatric hospital as I reflect of my nine years of experience, it became apparent that I have learnt and experienced enough for my next assignment.

Self-encouragement and determination is a resolve of the heart.

If you are determined to make a difference, and do the things that make a difference you will eventually make a difference.

Good things do not come easy

Short cuts will cut your life short.

Those who look ahead move ahead.

Life is all about making an impact. In your life time strive to make an impact in your community.

Make friends and connect with people who are moving ahead of you in life.

If you can look around well you have come a long way in your life, made a lot of difference and realized a lot of success in life.

If you are my old friend, hurry up to reach out to me before I become a stranger to you.

Everything I am blessed with inspirations from God, that change my definition and interpretation of the world around me.

I thought I was stagnant and lonely until I looked around and noticed my children running around and my wife cooking.

## Chapter 2 - The Power to Receive

At 40 I resigned my Job to seek the Lord forever.

My ministry took a drastic rise to the top when the wisdom of God visited me with knowledge and understanding.

You will be a better person if you understand the characteristics of your personality – your mood swings attitudes and habits.

It is the seed of love you sow into the heart of a child and a woman that you reap in due time.

Love is not selfish, love share everything including the concealed secrets of the mind.

As long as you have a prayer life and a bible; you will never feel lonely, rejected and idle in the race of life.

When good friends disconnect from you, let them go, they might have seen something new in a different direction.

Confidence in yourself and in God is the only way to bring you out of captivity

Never train a child to waste his/her time.

The mind is the greatest assets of a great future.

You walk by common sense run by principles and fly by instruction.

Those who fly in flight of life fly alone.

Up in the air you are alone. No one can toll you accept the compass of knowledge and information

I have seen a tolling vehicle I have seen a tolling ship I have never seen a tolling airplane.

I exercise my judgment and make a decision every minute of the day.

Decisions are crucial, critical and vital with reference to your future.

So many people wish for a great future. You can only work towards a great future.

Your celebrity status began when you discovered your talent. What are you good at? Work at it with all commitment.

Prayers will sustain you but the wisdom of God will prosper you.

When I met Oyedepo, his teachings changed my perspective, but when I met Ibiyeomie; His teaching changed my perception.

I will be successful in ministry if only I concentrate and focus my energy in the work of the ministry.

It took the late Dr. Vincent Pearle Norman's book to open my mind towards kingdom success.

# CHAPTER 3

# PRAYER OF SALVATION

I am glad you have read this book all the way from the beginning to this point. All I have said from the beginning will remain a mystery until you commit it into practice.

And before you do so I want you, if you have not given your life to Jesus to do so now. Give your life to Christ. I want you to know the truth! The truth is that Jesus died for your sins and because He died you must be alive and prosperous.

### What must I do to determine my divine visitation?

To determine divine visitation you must be born again. The word says as many as received him, to them gave He power to become the sons of God. Even to them that believe on his name.

To qualify for divine visitation do the following sincerely,

1) Acknowledge that you are a sinner and that He died for you. **Rom3:23.**

2) Repent of your sins. **Acts 3:19, Luke13:5, 2Peter3:9**

3) Believe in your heart that Jesus died for your sin. **Romans10:10**

4) Confess Jesus as the Lord over your life. **Romans10:10, Acts2:21**

**Now repeat this Prayer after me**

Say Lord Jesus, I accept you today, as my Lord and my savior, forgive me of my sins wash me with your blood. Right now, I believe, I am sanctified, I am save, I am free, I am free from the Power of sin to serve the Lord Jesus. Thank you Lord for saving me. Amen.

## Congratulation:
## YOU ARE NOW A BORN AGAIN CHRISTAIN

**AGAIN I SAY TO YOU CONGRATULATION**

## Chapter 3 - Prayer of Salvation

I adjure you to watch the Spirit of God bear witness with your Spirit confirming His word with signs following. The word says The Spirit itself beareth witness with our spirit, that we are the children of God.

## MIRACLE CARE OUTREACH

*"...But that the members should have the same care one for another"* **1cor12:25**

We are all members of the body of Christ. Jesus commanded us to love our neighbor as ourselves. This includes caring for one another as a member of one body. True love is expressed in caring and giving. The word says for God so Love He gave….

Reach out to someone in need of Jesus, help someone in crisis find Christ. Look out and prove your love to Jesus by caring and inviting your friends and associates to find Jesus the Healer.

Invite your friends to our Home Care Cell Fellowship (Miracle chapel Intl Satellite fellowship) In the USA at 33 Schley Street Newark New Jersey 07112.

If you are in Nigeria—**MIRACLE OF GOD MINISTRIES**

**A.K.A "MIRACLE CHAPEL INTL" Mpama –Egbu-Owerri Imo state Nigeria.**

(Home Care Cell fellowship Group). We meet every Tuesday at 6:00pm-7:00pm.

**LIFE IS NOT ALL ABOUT DURATION BUT ITS ALL ABOUT DONATION**

**What does the above statement mean?....**

*"Life consists not in accumulation of material wealth.."* **Luke 12:15.**

*"But it's all about liberality....meaning- what you can give and share with others."* **Proverb 11:25.**

## Chapter 3 - Prayer of Salvation

When you live for others--You live forever- because you out live your generation by the legacy you live behind after you depart into glory to be with the Lord. But when you live to yourself - you are reduced to self—you are easily forgotten when you die and depart in glory.

Permit me to admonish you today to live your life to be a blessing to a soul connected to you today. I want you to know that so many souls are connected and looking up to you, and through you so many souls will be saved and rescued from destruction. Will you disciple someone today to find Jesus Christ?

*"As a genuine Christian; it is your duty to evangelize Jesus Christ to all you meet on your way. Jesus is still in the healing business-Jesus is still doing miracles from time of old to now.*

*Therefore tell someone about Jesus Christ today, disciple and bring them to Church."*

**John 1:45 Philip findeth Nathanael....**

Please to prove the sincerity of your love for God today; please become a soul winner. The dignity of your Christianity is hidden in your boldness to proclaim and evangelize Jesus Christ to all you meet on your way.

There is a question mark on the integrity of your Christianity until you become a life soul winner. Invite someone to join us worship the Lord Jesus this coming Sunday.

**Amen**

Chapter 3 - Prayer of Salvation

# MIRACLE OF GOD MINISTRIES

## PILLARS OF THE COMMISSION

We Believe Preach and Practice the following,

1) We believe and preach Salvation to every living human being

2) We believe and preach Repentance and forgiveness of sins

3) We believe and preach the baptism of the Holy Spirit and Spiritual gifts

4) We believe and teach the Prosperity

5) We believe and preach Divine Healing and Miracles (Signs &Wonder)

6) We believe and preach Faith

7) We believe and Proclaim the Power of God (Supernatural)

8) We believe and Proclaim Praise& Worship to God

9) We believe and preach Wisdom

10) We believe and preach Holiness (Consecration)

11) We believe and preach Vision

12) We believe and teach the Word of God

13) We believe and teach Success

14) We believe and practice Prayer

15) We believe and teach Deliverance

**This 15 stones form the Pillars of Our Commission.**

Become part of this church family and follow this great move of God.

# MY HEART FELT PRAYER FOR YOU

It is my prayer that you develop a heart of love to God to give to your local assembly and to your local pastor.

## Chapter 3 - Prayer of Salvation

**Now let me Pray for you:**

*Almighty Father, open the eye of understanding of this precious love one reading this small book. Lord convict and compel them to become givers into your kingdom. I pray Lord that you use them to change the lives of others. I thank you for your merciful hand upon my life. I give you thanks for all my faithful giver. Father preserve them and keep them alive. I thank you and praise you.* **Amen.**

### *****Encounter with God******

Unless you are left alone you are not ready to encounter God. Jacob was left alone and he encountered God. I strongly urge you to create a quiet time with your God. A time of meditation and reflection. God is still omnipotent and all powerful. But you have to discover this by prayer and meditation in the word of God.

## Jacob encountered God

*"And Jacob was left alone; and there wrestled a man with him until the breaking of the day. And when he saw that he prevailed not against him, he touched the hollow of his thigh; and the hollow of Jacob's thigh was out of joint, as he wrestled with him. And he said, Let me go, for the day breaketh. And he said, I will not let thee go, except thou bless me. And he said unto him, What is thy name? And he said, Jacob. And he said, Thy name shall be called no more Jacob, but Israel: for as a prince hast thou power with God and with men, and hast prevailed."* **Genesis 32:24-28.**

## Apostle Paul encountered God

*"And as he journeyed, he came near Damascus: and suddenly there shined round about him a light from heaven: And he fell to the earth, and heard a voice saying unto him, Saul, Saul, why persecutest thou me? And he said, Who art thou, Lord? And the Lord said, I am Jesus whom thou persecutest: it is hard* for thee to kick against the pricks." **Acts 9:3-5**

# CHAPTER 4
## ABOUT THE AUTHOR

Rev Franklin N Abazie is the founding and Presiding Pastor of Miracle of God Ministries with headquarters in Newark, New Jersey USA and a branch church in Owerri- Imo State Nigeria. He is following the footsteps of one of his mentors, Oral Roberts (Healing Evangelist) of the blessed memory.

The Lord passed Oral Roberts healing mantle two days before he went to be with the Lord at age 91 into the hand of healing evangelist-Rev Franklin N Abazie in a vision.

In all his services the Power and Presence of God is present to heal all in his audience. He is an ordained man of God with a Healing Ministry reviving the healing and miracle ministry of Jesus Christ of Nazareth.

Pastor Franklin N Abazie, is called by God with a unique mandate:

*"THE MOMENT IS DUE TO IMPACT YOUR WORLD THROUGH THE REVIVAL OF THE HEALING & MIRACLE MINISTRY OF JESUS CHRIST OF NAZARETH.*

*I AM SENDING YOU TO RESTORE HEALTH UNTO THEE AND I WILL HEAL THEE OF THY WOUNDS. SAID THE LORD OF HOST"*

He is a gifted ardent Teacher of the word of God who operates also in the office of a Prophet, generating and attracting undeniable signs & wonders, special miracles and healings, with apostolic fireworks of the Holy Ghost.

He is the founding and presiding senior Pastor of this fast growing Healing ministry.

He has written over 86 inspirational, healing and transforming books covering almost all aspect of divine healing and life. He is happily married and blessed with children.

# BOOKS BY REV FRANKLIN N ABAZIE

1) Commanding Abundance
2) The outcome of faith
3) Understanding the secret of prevailing prayers
4) Understanding the secret of the man God uses
5) Activating my due Season
6) Overcoming Divine Verdicts
7) The Outcome of Divine Wisdom
8) Understanding God's Restoration Mandate
9) Walking in the Victory and Authority of the truth
10) Gods Covenant Exemption
11) Destiny Restoration Pillars
12) Provoking Acceptable Praise
13) Understanding Divine Judgment
14) Activating Angelic Re-enforcement
15) Provoking Un-Merited Favor
16) The Benefits of the Speaking faith
17) Understanding Divine Arrangement

18) Understanding Divine Healing
19) The Mystery of Endurance
20) Obeying Divine Instructions
21) Understanding the Voice of God
22) Never give up on Hope
23) The prevailing Power of faith
24) Understanding Divine Prosperity
25) The Reward of Prayer
26) Covenant Keys to Answered Prayers
27) Activating the Forces of Vengeance
28) Put your faith to work
29) Where is your trust?
30) The Audacity of the Blood of Jesus
31) Redeeming Your Days
32) The force of Vision
33) Breaking the shackles of Family Curses
34) Wisdom for Marriage Stability
35) The winners Faith
36) The Prayer solution
37) The power of Prayer
38) Prayer strategy
39) The prayer that works
40) Walking in Forgiveness
41) The power of the grace of God

42) The power of Persistence
43) Overcoming Divine verdicts
44) The audacity of the blood of Jesus.
45) The prevailing power of the blood of Jesus
46) The benefit of the speaking faith.
47) Fearless faith
48) Redeeming Your Days.
49) The Supernatural Power of Prophecy
50) The companionship of the Holy Spirit
51) Understanding Divine Judgement
52) Understanding Divine Prosperity
53) Dominating Controlling Forces
54) The winners Faith
55) Destiny Restoration Pillars
56) Developing Spiritual Muscles
57) Inexplicable faith
58) The lifestyle of Prayer
59) Developing a positive attitude in life.
60) The mystery of Divine supply
61) Encounter with God's Power
62) Walking in love
63) Praying in the Spirit
64) How to provoke your testimony

65) Walking in the reality of the Anointing
66) The reality of new birth
67) The price of freedom
68) The Supernatural power of faith
69) The Power of Persistence
70) The intellectual components of Redemption
71) Overcoming Fear
72) The Force of Vision
73) Overcoming Prevailing Challenges
74) The Power of the Grace of God
75) My life & Ministry
76) The Mystery of Praise

**MIRACLE OF GOD MINISTRIES**

NIGERIA CRUSADE 2012

**MIRACLE OF GOD MINISTRIES**

NIGERIA CRUSADE

2012

# MIRACLE OF GOD MINISTRIES

NIGERIA CRUSADE

2012

www.ingramcontent.com/pod-product-compliance
Lightning Source LLC
Chambersburg PA
CBHW021444080526
44588CB00009B/673